Write Short NonFiction Kindle Books Quickly

Make Money With Kindle Writing Nonfiction Books

By Bansari Parikh

Published By:

PB Publication

©Copyright 2015 – PB Publication

ISBN-13: 978-1511684699
ISBN-10: 1511684690

Table of Contents

Chapter 1:
Why Writing Short Non-Fiction Kindle Books

Holding on to the old mind sets is a risky point. Advancement and change is all around us, and also as the self-publishing world continues to obtain momentum, it is essential for authors to continue to be fast on their feet and also versatile. The capacity to shift gears and move quickly is among the great points that sets agile self-publishers different from the slow-moving giants of big publishing. With the best attitude, you could use that to your advantage in astonishing ways.

The idea that a book has to be this substantial, all- incorporating tome that supplies a definitive deluge of information on an offered subject is stagnant. It's messy much like the aged print publications sitting unblemished on your rack. I'll confess that some readers – even myself do still find a specific worth in longer works that provide a wide deep study in subject of interest. Yet the moments, innovations, and also fads of reading are changing with an accelerating pace.

With the Kindle boom skyrocketing the growth of the e-book market in recent times, much has actually transformed in the way people check out publications. You can now bring dozens, hundreds, also thousands of digital books with you in your pocket, thanks to e-readers as well as cell phone reading applications. Yet also as our virtual libraries and also reading possibilities remain to broaden, many find it's getting difficult as well as tougher to sit through longer non-fiction publications to gain the ideas they require. That's why much shorter books out are a real boon in today's busy scenario.

Time And Attention Are In Short Supply

Having the ability to sit down for a lazy afternoon as well as overcome a traditional-length non-fiction book at a leisurely rate is a luxury that a great deal of readers just can not pay for often. Lot of people are stuck diving into books on their cell phones throughout day-to-day commutes, ploughing through a few chapters during lunch break, or catching quick checks out to fritter away time in short bursts.

Spare time for reading is limited to begin with, and also it doesn't help as there are so many various other forms of content all vying for our focus - whether it's games and movies or web surfing as well as social networks. Those who like to read will certainly find a way to carve out the time for it somehow, but shorter books provide 2 factors that can be exceptionally important to busy readers

1) Beneficial material at an appealing cost as well as
2) A bite-sized length that they could plough through in a single sitting.

The vast bulk of non-fiction readers move in the direction of new books because they wish to learn. Most frequently, they're finding information that will certainly help them pick up a new skill or let them overcome a barrier they're encountering in their personal or professional life. If your publication is well- created and also gives viewers the info they need to help solve a pushing issue they're having problem with, they'll discover value in your work as well as appreciate it regardless of its length.

By reducing the additional fat as well as front-loading your short books with high quality material, your readers will love it. However lets not forget another very important piece of the puzzle below: rates.

The Pricing Factor And How It Affects Readers And Authors

In comparison to their longer-length print layout counterparts, Kindle books trend to the cheaper end of the pricing range – at least on the self-publishing side of things. Amazon.com's action of offering a 70 % royalty to KDP authors that price their books between $2.99 and $9.99

has actually had a tremendous effect on the marketplace.

From a reader's viewpoint, it's great to be able to acquire lots of digital books at such a low price. You can get a lot of excellent reads for a few bucks or much less, and also the on-demand nature of having the ability to look up a publication online, click a button, and also download it immediately gives an addicting level of instant gratification. You can develop a virtual library on a particular topic of passion for the price of a single print publication.

The huge range of variety has actually urged in the marketplace benefits every person as well. Personally, I enjoy to use my iPad, do a fast search on a specialized topic, download a book on it, and be reading it within minutes when I wish to learn something quickly.

Readers have an ever-growing variety of specialized books to select from, and authors have a lot more versatility to write in broader variety of niches. And also, people now care less concerning whether a book is self-published or traditionally published. While selecting a book at the nearby traditional book shops, I d simply acquire a handful of print books a year. Now? I get lots of e-books a year, support independent authors straight, as well as invest significantly less money and time in the process of doing this. I find still value in as well as support my neighborhood indie bookstores too, however the rates as well as availability of e- books is unbelievable to me as reader.

It's difficult to complain as a writer also, given that the significantly greater cut of the royalties from e- book sales under this plan overshadows anything you'll discover in conventional large publishing. Also the lower 35 % ball park royalty rate offered to writers which price their books less than $2.99 is still very nice and also you could price a great deal of books at an attractive $0.99 price point.

The $2.99 And Under Effect

Low cost and high royalties sounds like a win-win circumstance for everybody, right? In some ways they are, but there's a compromise here. Readers have grown accustomed with buying electronic publications at a considerably lower price point, making anything over the $4.99 variety a harder sell when there are so many fantastic eBooks available in the only $2.99 and also under wide range. Unless you're a big name writer or already have a huge well established audience, you're going to have a more difficult time making sales if you price your book outside of this range.

I'm just as guilty of this newer wave of buying mind set as the next book lover. Right here are some understandings into my thought process when I'm searching publications on the Kindle marketplace in "purchasing mode".

At $0.99? I don't even blink. If a publication interests me also a little and also has excellent testimonials, I'll purchase. For a dollar if it is even a little useful, I'll take into consideration that cash well spent.

At $2.99? I'm a little more attentive about

researching a publication, just what it covers, as well as whether it's suitable for what I'm trying to find. I'm still inclined to purchase if it looks suitable or captures my interest in other way.

Yet anything above $2.99? I hesitate. Why? Provided the high volume of publications I churn via in a provided month, I have to stick to a spending plan. This makes me far pickier about what publications I'll buy in the $4.99 as well as up at higher range. Considering recent book buying trends, I know I'm not the only one in this thinking.

So What Does This Mean For Authors?

If the marketplace demand and buying trends indicate that the majority of visitors are driven to simply want to pay, on average, a couple of bucks or much less for an eBook, that is very important to take note of. It changes the way authors need to think and work if we would like to achieve success.

As a writer, bringing a 50,000 to 75,000+ word eBook from concept to finalization and also persevering to an effective launch is a big endeavor. It could take lots of months, or even years, to create a work of that size, don't bother all the other editing and formatting costs entailed for a book of that length. Sometimes, it's worth going this route, but why pour all time and energy into creating one huge book that you can not cost a price point that'll justify the quantity of time as well as energy it took to create?

Keeping that exact same degree of efforts, you could compose and launch 5 to 10 much shorter eBooks as well as reap a considerably greater advantage in regards to visibility, readership, and sales. Of course, there's a lot even more to it than just "create shorter eBooks" as I'll describe in-depth in the approaching parts. However just before we venture down that course, it's worth having a look at several of the various other significant advantages that writers obtain from producing much shorter Kindle publications.

Chapter 2
HOW TO PICK THE BEST NICHE TO MAXIMIZE YOUR SALES

Choosing Your Niche

So, you would like to compose a book?

No, wait - you intend to write a bestselling book?

Fortunately is that it's less complicated now compared to before to write, publish and earn money from your words. Exactly how do I know? Because I have actually been making a fantastic living as a self-published writer for the last two years.

I do not have any sort of unique connections - I'm not a celebrity, neither do I have huge agents or publishing house marketing my work for me - yet I have actually been able to make use of the power of self-publishing to write and publish lot of bestselling books that supply me with a stable stream of easy income.

In this book, I will teach you everything that

can help you write, publish as well as make money from your work in few days.

What Is A Niche?

The first point you need to do is to pick your niche. A niche is merely a specific topic about which you want to write. It helps if you choose a particular niche that you delight in and also for which you have interest.

When it comes to writing, the more passion and expertise you have about a topic, the simpler the words will stream. You'll have less research to do as well as you could fill up the pages with every one of your smart ideas.

Some examples of subjects that I take pleasure in covering consist of:

- Public speaking
- Weight loss training
- Anti-procrastination methods for writers
- Relationship problems

You can write on any subject you wish. But before you could really start a publication you should comprehend the fundamental niche that works for you. Creating a book could help you become an authority on whichever topic you decide on.

This can branch off right into various other business areas within the same niche such as selling products, teaching programs, and also adding a brand name. This is one more reason you want to select sensibly - this could come to be a huge part of your working life.

How To Choose A Niche

You may currently know precisely what you would like to cover, however if you're unsure, there are a couple of points you can do to help you figure out the very best niche for you. Ask yourself a few key questions such as:

- Is there a topic on which I have a great deal of expertise?
- On what am I an expert?
- What topic or subjects hold my interest?
- What could I research and provide a "best of" to my viewers?
- Are there any kind of experts to which I have accessibility?

In my own life and experience. I know a lot

about public speaking. Therefore I have had the ability to write five very popular publications on it.

The internet marketer Tim Ferris knows a significant amount regarding outsourcing as well as building passive income. As a result he wrote in the book 'The 4-Hour' Job Week. It's best if you can write on a subject that truly matches your expertise. But perhaps you do not feel like an expert on any kind of topic. During that situation, you have alternatives.

One alternative is to end up being an expert in a topic that really passions you. If you're interested in something you'll be much more motivated to do research about it as well as share your interesting discoveries.

For example, you are really interested in success so you should research it and also have had the ability to share exactly what you have found out. You should read academic literary works on success and compile it with the study by writing a book.

Through the process of research you could come to be a specialist on practically any kind of subject. Yet you could additionally make use of resources such as specialists in the field. Today's social media sites make it easier to connect to specialists.

You would like to interview a couple of experts in a specific niche then distil their wisdom into bite-sized portions for your viewers. That's just what Napoleon Hill did in his book. "Think and grow

If you have accessibility to experts in a specific niche, that can lead your selection of topic. But if you do not have prompt access to professionals, don't allow that to stop you from attempting to get in touch with experts in an industry that intrigues you.

Most importantly, focus on writing a book that you 'd be interested in reading. If you aren't interested about book you're writing, your viewers probably will not.

Is There A Demand?

As soon as you have actually chosen a specific niche, it's important to view if there's a demand for it just before moving forward. You can do many things to evaluate the marketplace as well as figure out whether your book will be received favorably.

Initially, you can go to Amazon and search for titles on your subject. For instance, if you would like to compose on public speaking, you'll type" public speaking" in the search bar. Surf the category as well as search for a few signs.

Just how popular are the books in this classification? You could see by looking at the sales rank. You intend to look for books that have a sales rank of 25,000 or less. The lower the number, the greater the sales of book.

If you cannot locate at the very least 3 books with that low sales rank, it suggests there isn't much demand for your subject. Let's take a look at the example of procrastination as a particular niche. If I intended to create a book to assist folks battle procrastination, I would check with Amazon for books on procrastination.

If I locate that there are at least 3 books with

a ranking less than 25000, I can be sure that there's a need for this topic.

If you have the ability to create a good publication and also market it well, you will certainly generate income. For example, at the time, if we take a look at the example of "pet grooming" as niche we'll see something different. When you hunt for book on pet grooming you'll find that there aren't in the leading 25,000. The average sales ranking for a publication on pet grooming seems to float around 200,000 (which is an awful sales ranking!).

Even if pet grooming is your interest, it may not be the best particular niche because it merely will not market. There's not enough demand. Even if you write an excellent book, you could not make much cash on it.

If this takes place, return to Amazon.com as well as start researching Amazon Kindle books. You'll start to see which topics sell well as well as which do not. You would like to find topics that are selling well and that compare with your interests.

Udemy (https://www.udemy.com/) is one more resource to help you understand more about what's in demand. Udemy is a website that offers online learning courses. Presently the platform has more than 8,000 courses created by 4,000 independent course creators.

If you go to Udemy you could browse through the categories and also view what is prominent. As an example, go to the business category and also sort by "Popularity." This will certainly show you the most popular business course on platform.

When I visit Udemy now and do this search, I view a course called "Body Language for Business owners." This training course is selling for $199 and has more than 1,100 students. This tells me there is a high need due to the fact that a bunch of individuals are willing to pay a lot of money for this training course. Yes, several of those students could have received totally free coupons for the program, however I'm wagering that there are quite a lot of that paid the full price.

If I go back over to Amazon.com and execute a search, I find that BODY LANGUAGE by Joe Navarro - selling at $9.99 and also rated 3,861 in the Kindle Store.

The Definitive Book of Body Language by

Allan Pease - costing \$12.99 and rated 14,115 in the Kindle Store.

Body Language 101: The Ultimate Guide to knowing when people are lying, how they are feeling, what they are thinking and more by David Lambert - selling at \$0.99 and ranked 20,404 in the Kindle Store.

So as you can see, at least three books are ranked listed below 25,000 in this category. This is one more sign that "body language" is a prominent subject. One fascinating thing to note is that the 3rd book, Body Language 101, has a dreadful cover (no offense to the author) and approximately just three out of 5 stars in the review.

Narrowing Your Niche

Since you've done a little homework as well as investigated the niche regarding which you're interested in writing, you should limit your subject down. Let's take a look at exactly what that means and also why it is essential.

An individual new to writing on Kindle might choose to write a publication called How to Start a Business. This topic is preferred, but it's far as well wide. There are a couple of problems with this kind of publication.

Initially, there are currently a great deal of "how to start a business" books on Amazon. Yours will not seem any kind of different if you go with that title. Why would certainly any individual get your book instead of one that has been released by a big-five publishing house with a well-known writer?

Second, this subject would certainly take a long time to research and compose appropriately. It could take you hundreds of hours and hundreds of pages to cover every little thing. As well as the cost factor for Kindle books is usually in between $2.99 and $5.99. That would certainly be a lot of job to do for such a little revenue.

Ultimately, this title assures the readers too much. It's such an extensive subject that the viewers believe it will be the supreme quick guide for any type of company. When they download book they will have extremely high expectations.

There will inevitably be things that you didn't cover in your quick guide and also this will cause disappointment - as well as bad testimonials. And also as a result of bad reviews, sales numbers will plummet.

To prevent this calamity, you should limit your specific niche. You want to choose just ONE issue that your book can fix. It needs to be extremely clear as well as laser-targeted in order to make your visitors delighted.

For example, check out this book that you've purchased. It's not a book on How you can Publish a Book. Rather, it's 'Write a Short Non-Fiction Kindle Book Quickly'. As you could see, this is an extremely particular guide as well as has a particular target audience consisting of:

- Kindle writers
- Non-fiction publication authors
- Individuals curious about writing a book rapidly.

This does eliminate a bunch of individuals such as those who don't publish on Kindle, fiction writers, and those that don't concur that a publication written in few days can be of top quality. But that's actually a good thing!

I discover that only the right readers buy my publications.

That indicates I have a lesser risk of unfavorable assessments from an extreme visitor who expected something different. It also assists my book to stand apart from the competitors.

My book instantly draws the readers who would be interested in it but not so generic. And because I've focused on resolving only one or two issues in my publication I don't have to write hundreds of pages on the topic.

My book will be more focused and also it will certainly be much shorter, making it a far better choice to price it at $2.99. Now if I compose 2 or 3 of these shorter publications, I could put them with each other in a package and also market them at a larger cost.

This allows my devoted followers to get a wonderful savings on the plan. It makes it easier for my viewers to recognize what they're obtaining and find worth in the books. For me it implies even more cash than if I simply wrote one large book on Ways to Publish a Book.

Niche Task

Since you have read through this chapter you might feel your very own wheels starting to transform. Your job list for today, is to identify your specific niche. You have to see to it that you:

- Decide on a niche that interests you
- Study the need for your specific niche
- Limit your niche to ensure that your publication is extremely focused on just one issue or obstacle you could resolve.

Chapter 3
FOUR COMMON TYPES OF SHORT KINDLE BOOKS YOU CAN WRITE

Few writers delight in to stick with writing the specific very same type of book repeatedly again. I do not blame them. It's a lot of fun to switch over points up now and then, as well as your certain format and also method to every book you compose could make a big distinction in how smoothly all of it comes together.

Specific viewers are more drawn in to various sorts of non-fiction styles also, so experimenting to get to brand-new audiences can be beneficial in that regard. If you're thinking about altering points up and also can utilize some suggestions, below are some of the much more usual styles of non-fiction publications that lend themselves to short book format.

All Interview-Focused Book

Writing from your own personal encounter with a topic is easy, but often you might intend to tap other experts in your given industry to obtain their recommendations as well as point of view to weave throughout your book. Interviews are an excellent method to add worth to your book and bulk up your very own ideas with other peoples' expert views.

Finding, arranging, conducting, and also transcribing job interviews could be tedious work that takes added time to pull together, yet they usually generate outstanding material that makes it worth the initiative. The other upside is you can swiftly generate a high volume of material with only a handful of interviews, making it very easy to put a great book with each other once you collect all that you need to compose it up.

A List Book Or Tip Book

Lists books can be extremely simple to create, as well as they're rather preferred among readers. Whether you're writing a book of suggestions or a collection of intriguing as well as insightful nuggets (like the probably completely imaginary 10 Outstanding Real life Mysteries) their length is defined by the number of products you plan to include.

You could write a book that invests even more time dedicated to going over a smaller sized variety of list items in greater depth, or string together a much larger number of short and punchy entries. Developing wonderful pointers or listing things is the hardest component, but once you acquire a great list together as well as organize it well, these books appear to all but create themselves.

A Book That Answers A Specific Question

Short books are excellent for narrowing down as well as honing-in on a single streamlined topic. Sometimes, that boils down to providing a deep dive answer to a single concern. A publication on the best ways to properly format Kindle books is one example. A book on how to increase your writing speed is another. If you commonly get asked the very same inquiry by bunches of different readers, that must set your authorial Feeling tingling. Why not cook up an eBook-length answer to a burning question your audience has?

A Long-Form Article Book

Long-form journalism is a perfect for the brief Kindle book format. It's a pairing that makes a lot of sense when you take into consideration the quantity of interviewing and reporting that goes into crafting a sound feature article. A huge chunk of that hard work gets left on the cutting room flooring, as well, as you trim everything down to suit within your editor's suggested word matter. Why not consider creating an extensive article in short book style? An increasing number of journalist-turned-authors are doing it. Imagine the ground you can cover, from fad items and also cultural records to quirky profiles and more. These are simply a few concepts to get you started. Broaden your mind-set, and also view what kind of distinct publication suggestions you could think of!

Chapter 4
THE QUICK & EASY
METHOD FOR MAKING
YOUR BOOK

Why Create An Outline?

An Outline being the framework or overview of your book, is necessary to the writing procedure for a few different reasons. First, an outline helps you to know the framework as well as direction of your publication. Eventually, having a synopsis will aid you to write faster.

When you have your framework completed prior to you begin writing, you'll have the ability to prevent blank page syndrome. When it's time to take a seat at your desk to compose your book, you'll never ever have to handle writer's block.

With an overview you could understand exactly what it is you want to write. Moreover you can create a publication that moves from subject to subject in an organized way that your visitors will also appreciate.

For a long period of time I hated outlining my books. I believed that it was ridiculous and also a waste of time. I assumed that I can dive directly into writing as well as allow my concepts magically be delivered from my head to the page. Nonetheless, I rapidly figured out that didn't function as well as I anticipated.

The outline is a tool that imitates a bridge between your head and the page. The suggestions are already in your head; however the overview could offer you a clear, structured path to writing your concepts as well as creating a good book.

Outlining Made Simple

Your synopsis does not have to be a laborious activity. In fact, you can swiftly outline your publication in an easy process. Right here's how I do it:

Initially, I develop a new paper titled "Synopsis." In this document, I create a Table of Contents and after that I develop sample chapter titles. For example, for this publication I produced the chapter titles "Select Your Niche," "Common types of short books," and "Creating an Outline.".

Example:

1. Why to write short Non-Fiction book.

2. Select your Niche.

3. Common Types of Short Books.

4. Creating an Outline.

5. Creating Title.

You'll discover I'm not trying to come up with elegant titles nor I over think the procedure. I am simply conceptualizing my feasible chapter titles.

Considering that many non-fiction publications have a detailed logical process, your chapters will additionally follow that sort of series.

After you've written your feasible chapter titles, have a look at the Table of Contents as well as see if it makes logical sense. You might find that you should relocate a few of them around so that the book flows nicely in a logical order.

Add Main Points

When you have your table of contents fleshed out, you could include even more information. For every chapter you would like to include a couple of main points. In my very own process I include in bullet points that are the three to six bottom lines, stories, or instances I wish to cover in that chapter.

1. **Why to write short Non-Fiction book.**
   - ➤ **Readers have less time.**
   - ➤ **Short eBooks preferred over long books.**
   - ➤ **Low Pricing.**
2. **Select your Niche.**
   - ➤ **What Is a Niche?**
   - ➤ **How to Choose a Niche**
   - ➤ **Demand for Niche**
3. **Common Types of Short Books.**
   - ➤ **All Interview-Focused Book**
   - ➤ **A List Book Or Tip Book**
   - ➤ **Book That Answers A Specific Question**
   - ➤ **Long-Form Article Book**

I do not fret about making an in-depth outline. This is merely a quick skeletal system of the book that reveals me what the general publication will certainly cover. I can consistently recognize what to create next as well as I could keep the organization and also flow of the book consistent. And that's it!

All Evolving Outline

One essential thing to note is that as you compose, your overview will develop. The outlining part takes place, at the same time as your research phase. As you study as well as discover even more information, your mind will certainly be creating an outline.

It makes sense, after that, to go ahead and also dump this details right into a Word file, or at the very least write it down on paper. In this manner you don't have to remember just what you intend to include - it's already there for you in an outline form.

After you finish the research study phase, though, you'll want to commit one day particularly to your outline. You'll want to make certain that your overview is full and also extensive. Before you start writing, you need to feel happy with just what it will contain.

Chapter 5
HOW TO CRAFT POWERFUL BOOK TITLES THAT GENERATE SALES

Titles

Now that you have created the framework of your book, you're possibly all set to start writing. But wait! You're not quite there yet. Typically, with traditional publishing, that's exactly what you'd do. Nevertheless, with non-fiction Kindle publications I advise a different technique.

As a Kindle author you are accountable for everything in the publication procedure - from the writing to the editing to the cover layout. That suggests there's a great deal to think of while you're putting your book with together.

With Kindle publishing, authors reside in an amazing age where any individual could make money from their words - and I imply anybody. It's just a concern of complying with the appropriate steps that are recommended in this guide and then duplicating them repeatedly with as numerous books as possible.

You could not earn hundreds or thousands of dollars for each book, however each publication could effortlessly put a couple hundred additional dollars in your pocket each month. So the more books you write over time, the greater your income will certainly be.

Title Creation Saves Time

I am especially interested about producing top quality eBooks in a short amount of time. As a result of that, I've developed a group of professional editors and also designers who assist me with my books.

I have a cover designer that designs superb eBook covers for me. I also have a team of 2 editors which edit as well as help improve my publications to guarantee they review well. It is necessary to have an additional set of eyes to read your material - you see it so much that you might miss errors or things that make good sense to you yet would be perplexing to somebody else.

This help is invaluable, but each of these people will take a few days to finish the work I give them. So in order to accelerate the process, I like to insure that I reduce the wait time to as short as feasible.

By developing the book title prior to I start writing my book, I can then outsource it to my designer. By doing this, my cover designer can be thinking of new styles for the book while I start creating the book.

I used to wait until I was finished writing to

think of titles for my books. Nonetheless, this brought in a minimum of a week of waiting time for the cover to come back. After I completed the writing, I would certainly invest 1 day brainstorming titles. Then I would provide the title to my designer and await as much as a week while he developed the cover designs. Now, I can accelerate the process by producing the title initially. Obviously, if speed isn't your key issue you can wait till you've finished writing.

Developing The Title

How long should it take to produce a title? Not long at all. It really shouldn't take greater than a number of hrs. I prefer to start brainstorming my title on the day I finish the synopsis for my book.

This is a good time to brainstorm because you've currently:

- Chosen your specific niche
- Had a look at competition on Amazon
- Collected the study
- Created an outline
- Figured out the function of the book

From your study, you'll recognize what readers need and just what benefits you can provide them. All you need to do, then, is to produce a title that lets your possible readers recognize that your book can fix their issues.

The Importance Of A Great Title

If you really want a best-selling publication, you cannot underestimate the power of the title. As an example, think about the tale of Emanuel Hardeman Julius.

Hardeman Julius was an American writer which published his work during the early 20th century.

In merely twenty years, he marketed more than 200 million publications. If you consider the time duration, you'll recognize how successful he was.

But a bunch of his success can be associated with his book titles - as well as his distinctive method of testing them. He would in fact release the same books under different titles and figure out which sold better.

For example, his publication labeled The Mystery of the Iron Mask sold approximately 11,000 copies a year. Nonetheless, the same publication with the title The Mystery of the Man in the Iron Mask was a lot more successful, selling over 30,000 duplicates in a solitary year.

Both of these books were identical tales. The only distinction was the title - and that made all the difference when it pertained to sales.

For instance, his publication Casanova and His Love offered a decent 8,000 copies. Yet when he altered the title to Casanova, History's Greatest Lover the book marketed more than 22,000 copies.

One of the most successful title modifications was for his book Art of Controversy. With this title it sold precisely no copies in a year. But when he relabeled it How to Argue Logically, it offered greater than 30,000 copies. Once more, exact same book, just a different title

What Makes A Great Title?

There are several elements that can help to make your title wonderful. Titles for non-fiction publications must be relatively easy. Right here's what you really want:

1. A title that clearly conveys the benefit of your publication to your visitors.

2. A title and also subtitle that contain the key words your Amazon visitors would utilize when searching for books on your topic.

Let's take a look at the procedure of establishing your title in much more detail. You want your primary title to be 10 words or less. This isn't really a set rule, yet a standard that I advise. You can most definitely develop a title that is longer and also have success.

But I discover that a brief title with a longer caption is the combination that works ideal on Amazon. There are two kinds of brief titles that seem to do well: benefit titles and curiosity titles.

Benefit Titles

The 1st type of title clearly determines just what the book has to do with and also the benefits that visitors expect from it. I call these "benefit titles."

When you're writing your very own title, you have to ask on your own:

What does this publication offer my visitors? What problem does it help them to fix? What will reading this book allow the readers to accomplish?

After that, in less than 10 words, produce a title that plainly as well as merely shows this. Below are a couple of title design templates that can help you get started:

How to (bring in benefit here: e.g., "Write Non Fiction eBooks in 15 Days").

How to (bring in perk below: e.g., "Reduce weight Rapidly") Without (add discomfort here: e.g., "Needing to Diet ").

23 Ways to (include advantage below: e.g., "Promote Your Non-Fiction eBook Online").

10 Days to (include benefit here: e.g., "A Swimwear Body").

How I (add your success story: e.g.,

"Elevated Myself from Failure to Success in Sales").

These are just a couple of instances for producing your very own eBook title. The essential thing is that if you opt for this type of title, it needs to be clear, straightforward, and also guarantee your viewers something of value.

Curiosity Titles

The 2nd kind of titles is curiosity titles. These make you wonder about something and also ignite your passion. Some examples consist of:

Becoming the 1 % by Dennis Crosby (Makes you wonder, "Becoming the 1 %? Exactly what does that imply?").

E-Squared by Pam Grout (Makes you wonder, "Hmm, what's that concerning?").

Hooked by Nir Eval (Makes you question, "Hooked to just what?").

While such titles can attract reader curiosity, on their own they can be perplexing. To be effective, they should have benefit-driven captions. The title gets your interest, however the subtitle informs you what book is truly about.

Brainstorming Your Own Book Title

Since you have actually learned a little bit concerning what makes a best-selling title, it's time to start working with your very own title. Below is what I suggest you do:

Know Your Audience

Assume carefully about who your actual readers are. Just what is their # 1 discomfort point? What trouble are they aiming to address? What benefit does your publication supply them? Why would they acquire your book?

Create A Spider Map

After you've really spent time thinking of your audience, snatch a piece of paper and also write the word 'Title' in the middle of the page. Circle that word. This composes the" body" of your spider.

Now begin creating your spider's "legs" by documenting as several possible titles as you can, branching off from your circle. Spend Thirty Minutes doing this. Do not stress over whether your ideas are good or not.

This isn't a time to judge your concepts - that will really stop the flow of imagination. At this point, no concept is a bad one. At the end of half an hour you can choose the one you think works best. Or you find that placing a number of ideas with each other functions well.

Have A Title Party

If you're still in need of a great title, you could have a title event. Invite as several close friends as you could over for dinner. It's great if they're in your target customer base, however they definitely don't need to be for this to work.

Have pizza and drinks, or whatever your good friends like. After that take Thirty Minutes to let every person know what your publication is about and also ask to assist you create some suggestions for titles.

Ask people to shout their responses and write them down on a large piece of paper. Once again, don't evaluate the concepts, merely write them down. This gives you much more alternatives. After the half hour, you could go back to your social occasion with your buddies.

Chapter 6
OUTSOURCING

In order to earn a living from writing, you should like to write. Without that enthusiasm, you just can't keep it for the quantity of time needed to make it work.

If you write a book a week you can write about 52 books a year. That's a great deal of work and also a substantial amount of writing. You could wear out or miss a week occasionally, so give shake room and also reduced estimations when time-lining your book production. If you write 2 book a month, that's 24 books a year.

For those intending to earn a living at writing, it should be a full time job and that's a little bit difficult to do when progression is so slow. Also at the crazy speed of a book a week, you're not going to make a lot, not also at the end of the initial year.

That's where outsourcing is available, also known as ghost writing. When you outsource your book writing you can quickly double, triple, or quadruple your writing rate. Writing two books a month now comes to be 4 books a month, or perhaps six or eight depending on how you make use of outsourcing.

You can make your target of 80 books possible in 6 months or less while maintaining quality, if you worked at it.

The outsourced author for your book has to have talent to write, however the material and also style they write should be created by you.

Your book should be thoroughly mapped and outlined by you. For nonfiction book, where study has to be done, you can give a listing of authorized sources such as "only studies in these certain journals," or offer accessibility to sites that require paid solutions to access the details to the outsourced writer.

The style for your nonfiction writing should be your style, as well. If you are writing a book on the best ways to reduce weight, you would certainly supply the outsourcer with a rundown that can look like this:

Chapter Title (Drink Lots of Water).

Present the idea (We are made of primarily water, while we could survive a month or more without food we could only do so for a couple of day without water ...).

Any sort of history (If you're into Paleo diet, your only option is water! ...).

Any kind of research information (website no more than 3 sturdy relevant studies in between water and weight reduction ...).

Press subject importance (Water is a organic, healthy and balanced means to slim down ...).

Sub-topic 1 (Water can be made use of to substitute for other kinds of drinks, specifically sweet and salty' ones ...).

Sub-topic 2 (Water loads the belly, making you really feel full. So, drink a glass prior to your lunch & dinner and also one after to keep that full sensation so you don't overeat ...).

Conclusion (summary and also recap of main point ...).

I find it good to give an example of or write out an example of a chapter or section in book I want them to write. I will frequently write a complete section or subchapter for the outsourced writer to use as an overview. Your design could be to mix in research studies or other little details directly into the sub-topics. You may want to provide the author the section topic along with the sub-topics, or none in any way. Nevertheless, the more information the better.

The suggestion isn't really to have someone else simply write a random book that you then turn around and also market. It must be an expansion of your writing.

You desire your vision as well as creativity to be carried out in full.

The cost for the outsourcer can be anywhere from a hundred to $200+ depending on the outsourcer and length of the book. For nonfiction, a book between 5K as well as 10K words will certainly work.

Negotiate and request for sample material

Do a hunt for outsourcing, ghost writer, and freelance writing to discover hundreds of people looking for your business. Several of individuals you contact work as group or small business that has many authors helping them. They make a lot of money. On places like eLance, their profile blog posts how much they have actually gained. It's not uncommon to find ghost writers making half a million to numerous million selling their services. That's a great deal of publications being published by other people! Small companies that utilize a few ghost writers can make millions a year. It allows business as well as numerous self-publishers are capitalizing on the solutions.

Just about every book makes a profit, some do it after the first month while others do it after six months or more. It depends on how marketable the book is.

It's difficult to do what you like to do when you can't sustain yourself doing it! Outsourcing is the answer for self - publishers who are new to make a living from writing.

Chapter 7
YOUR FIRST DRAFT IS DONE. NOW WHAT?

Few milestone of the book writing process are as satisfying as wrapping up your initial completed draft. You've been striving, pushing on your own to crank out words on a daily basis, as well as coming closer to a finished publication with every action. You ultimately complete it up, and it really feels GREAT! You have actually written a publication - or at least something approximately book-like. But now what?

The very best point you can do right now, at this actual minute when you're overflowing with bliss over your accomplishment, is to keep your manuscript aside and forget it that it exist ... if only a while. I understand, it is difficult, however give your publication some breathing space as well as allow it simmer in its very own first daftness.

Let me clarify why this is so crucial.

It's alluring to run a quick spell check, give it a read-through, make a few quick modifications, and stop. Many writers are eager to get their work out into the world that they rush with the self -editing (and appropriate editing) procedure in an initiative to have actually a finished book, but you have to hang around honing your rough book to make it the best before you could give it to an editor.

Wait, aren't editors expected to make your job better and also discover all the junk you missed out on? Isn't really that why you're hiring them in the first place? Yes as well as no. True: that's exactly what they exist to do to an extent, yet you can not simply dump a stack of sloppy copy in their lap and also anticipate them to transform it right into gold for you. First and foremost, the burden of writing a terrific book is on you. You ought to do everything you could to see to it your composition is as tidy as well as cleaned-up as feasible before it gets sent along for a formal edit.

This surpasses checking for grammar and also punctuation slips. You have to look at tone, consistency, flow, the material itself, and tons of various other important factors that contribute to your work's worth. Often an initial draft will certainly turn out outstanding on the very first go around. Usually, however, it'll still need a lot of work to get it anywhere near where it should be just before it's ready for a correct edit.

Do not try to dig into the fine-tuning procedure if you've simply finished your draft. It's still very much fresh at that point. You'll be way to close to the work to be able to assess it and make the hard choices as well as changes that should be made in order to enhance on it. For that, you have to give it time and also space. Trust me: this distance is essential.

I'll often take a final draft for anywhere between a few weeks to a couple of months if required. Meanwhile, I focus on other tasks and also try to distance myself from the draft as long as possible just before I open it back up for another look. Though you might intend to keep production process moving so you can push closer to release, this is one step you should not hurry.

Returning to your manuscript after you've had enough space to detach from it lets you see it through fresh eyes. You'll catch much more errors, be more in harmony with any section that could appear like they need revamping, and - essential of all - be a lot more ready for the suggestion of cutting out bad bits and changing anything that's off.

When you've let your composition breath long enough, it's time to roll up your sleeves for another go!

The Phases Of Editing

Modifying your book needs to always be a multi-stage procedure. The more passes as well as closer examination you offer it, the even more chances you'll have to repair any kind of issues and also make crucial improvements that'll give you a much more professional looking product. To complete that, you'll wish to spend lots of your own time reading and also remodeling the composition till it's first-class, get comments from beta visitors that can help form your later drafts, then lastly hire a professional editor to spit shine the final draft. Right here's a better look at each stage of the editing procedure.

Self-Editing Your Work

After you have actually detached from your first draft as well as allow it sit for a while, you ought to reach a point where it's safe to dive back into it without being attached to the book. You need to be prepared to put down the red ink, trim the awful little bits, and highlight the ugly flaws throughout your manuscript. That's a lot easier to do when you're not still in the clutches of your own words and writing.

The very first pass has the tendency to be the messiest, as lots of areas of your publication may still be quite harsh. You could discover whole chapters that have to be re-written or re-arranged, and it's possible you could also discover even bigger troubles that need to be resolved. You'll discover a lot about what works and what does not in your publication. That's all great and to be expected. Remember that you're working with your "puke draft" right here. It's not suggested to be pretty at this point, it merely exist-so you can refine it into something amazing.

As frustrating as discovering bigger concerns can be, it's far better to discover them now while you're in fixing and polishing mode than to allow them glide as well as wait until viewers have a chance to tear your book apart in Amazon assessments.

Begin your self-editing procedure with a standard read-through. Some authors publish out their composition and also mark it up by hand. Others work directly on their computer systems or read their work loud. I choose to send a digital variation of my draft to my Kindle account so I could download and install and review it on my iPad - much like I would with the finished product. This lets me make use of the app's highlight and note taking functions to mark up the draft.

You could utilize any one of these techniques or design your own, though it is good to vary your strategy with each pass you take, since that can aid you capture things you missed.

When sitting down to read your vomit draft for the initial time, focus entirely on book instead of making changes as you go. Take comprehensive notes and highlight any issues you find, but don't attempt to make all of the edits right then and there. It's a sure thing that there will certainly be several issues. Get through reading and markup initially, after that you can take a seat to make changes later.

Five Things To Watch Out For

As you read your work with a critical eye and an open mind, below are some of the many things you should do.

- Cohesion and Flow
- Does every little thing make good sense as you review it, as well as does it stream well?
- Look out for any stretches that bog you down or lull the drive.
- Dense paragraphs that are long and words act like speed bumps for visitors. Much shorter graphs as well as generous use of subheads separate the walls of text as well as keep folks reading at a constant rate.

If you're battling to read a specifically dense passage as well as are dying to skip in advance, it's secure to think that your readers are apt to feel the same way. Change points around keep your visitors involved. Take a look at your publication all at once. Don't hesitate to relocate things around if items match better in other places in your book than where you first placed them.

Does your book grab readers and also hook their interest from the get go? Pay attention to your intro, table of contents, and also opening up chapters. Make every little thing stylish and luring, since nothing will avert potential buyers much faster than placing them to sleep just before they even make it through the very first couple of paragraphs.

This is two times as essential with much shorter Kindle publications. Amazon.com's "Look Inside" preview function lets prospective customers browse roughly the very first 10 percent of your publication. Numerous readers will take a pass if you can not hook them early on. Make the most of this indispensable real estate by setting the ideal tone and ensuring your product attracts viewers in right at the starting line.

(a) Facts And Figures

If you point out certain truths, figures, as well as various other important data throughout your book, it's absolutely worth taking the time to check to make sure they're both exact and also as updated as possible before your book launches.

You must likewise be careful when it includes any type of present information or figures that could alter in the near future, dating your book in the process. This will certainly require you to update it often to remain current, which can be a pain if it's a figure that changes too often.

Be on the lookout for anything else that appears a little bit suspicious. Mark it for later on when you have time to look it up as well as ensure everything is correct. Furthermore, if you quote experts you have actually interviewed, it's not a bad suggestion to check any strong cases they make that will certainly show up in your book.

(b) Spelling And Grammar

Typos and also bad grammar will certainly sink your Kindle book faster than a wild wombat gnawing an opening in your kiddy swimming pool. Readers on the Kindle market tend to get rankled by punctuation and also grammar concerns they locate in books - and rightly so! They're not shy concerning knocking a few stars off terribly modified books when they rate them on the market either, so this is one area you have to be careful. It's true. Typos happen. Even pro-edited books from big publication wind up with issues, but that's no excuse to be lazy about your writing. Do every little thing in your power to make your book tidy and also mistake free, and you will increase your opportunity of making favorable reviews. One tip: don't trust your spellchecker. It won't capture every little thing, and also simple misses like a "they're" rather than "their" can make a big distinction.

(c) Fluff And Junk Words

Keep a vigilant watch for unnecessary fluff as well as junk writing. The more you write as well as publish, much better you'll get at cutting the fluff from your work. Novice writers are occasionally vulnerable to cushioning their work with content that fills up space yet does not really claim much or offer value to readers. Work on pointing this when you see it, and be willing to cut this out to tighten up your writing. Your readers (and publishers) will value it.

(d) Tone And Consistent Voice

A lot of writers create a distinct tone to their work over time as they discover their voice. You may not be as knowledgeable about your very own creating voice as your readers will be, but reviewing your work by, the self-editing procedure will aid you give a good feeling for it. While your tone can and will certainly change from book-to-book depending on the customer base you're creating for, it is very important to make sure your voice corresponds throughout your book or it could toss visitors for an unwanted loop.

History being a matter of plain consistency, the sort of tone you make use of is vital. Try to stay clear of using profanity, being too much negative, or writing in a manner that could irritate your audience base or create an unfavorable response.

(e) Content

One last thing to consider out as you review your book as well as make several self-editing passes is the worth as well as scope of the material you've produced. Reviewing your book from beginning to end can be fairly unveiling, as well as it's frequently the only means to determine exactly how on-point you are with your job. Did you cover all the ground you would like to cover? Is something missing out on that you should include? Did you stuff sufficient value right into the work to keep viewers delighted? These are all critical things to think about, because now is the time to make any type of significant architectural changes to your publication just before you send it off for others to check out.

Watch each one of these things every single time you review your draft and make any kind of required changes. I recommend you come close to self-editing as a multi-phase procedure. Take at the very least three passes - checking out your work from beginning to end, making notes, and afterwards executing adjustments with each pass. Every modifying pass you make need to concentrate on finding and repairing all of the key points discussed over, yet there's a reason for doing at least 3 rounds of self-editing.

In the first go-around, you'll truly want to concentrate on making any kind of big sweeping modifications to your draft and sniffing out anything that's off with your task. If your vomit draft needs any serious revamping, this is where you'll intend to explore it. This first time will certainly be the longest as well as most grueling, however braving this initial onslaught and seeing it through alive makes subsequent passes a whole lot simpler.

Your target in the second round of self-editing is to see to it any kind major changes you made to the composition in your first pass blends well with the rest of the material. As you resolve any one of those kinks, you still would like to watch for points you missed. With each pass, expect to find brand-new things to modify, but your general quantity of heavy-duty tinkering needs to taper down with each run.

Round 3 is about capturing any sticking around typos and also grammar problems while spit-shining your work so it pops. Here, you may swap out a few words, discover a couple of typos, and make small fixes to the composition. At this point, you should be finished with the bulk of the hefty lifting and concentrating on only making small adjustments to the text.

As soon as you get your manuscript as spick-and-span as you could get it, and you sense that not much more you can do to improve on it, that's when it's time to see exactly what others think. Some writers skip straight to working with an editor, which is great, but spending a little time acquiring feedback from beta viewers can be rewarding.

Chapter 8
HIRING A PROFESSIONAL EDITOR – WITHOUT GOING BROKE

Send Your Book To An Editor

After editing your own publication, you may be lured to post it straight to Amazon, however I extremely dissuade this. Why? Because even if you have a wonderful eye for information, you may miss out on some noticeable blunders given that you created the book.

Your mind has a tendency to overlook mistakes that you have actually made. It's important, then, to send it to a professional editor. This will keep you from acquiring unfavorable testimonials as a result of ridiculous errors that might have been quickly prevented.

The Benefits Of Hiring A Professional Editor

Working with an expert editor could help to insure that your work is devoid of mistakes. A specialist can carefully examine your book and fix any kind of grammatical or structural errors you have actually made.

For my own books, my editor plays a vital role in success. She polishes up the quality of my writing so that I can write much faster. Let me discuss.

She spent a few days evaluating my book as well as correcting my mistakes. After that I sent the book to an additional editor, just in case my initial editor had actually missed out on anything. I got a much more enhanced version back within a few days.

Following this procedure, I was able to finish the entire writing, modifying as well as publishing process much quicker than it would certainly have taken otherwise.

It Takes A Team

If you want to earn money from your words, you need to view writing as an art along with a business. To run business you should make some investments. It helps to work with clever folks who excel at just what they do.

What if I don't have sufficient cash to hire an editor? Can't I merely ask my friends and also family members that can help me edit my publication?" Unless your friends and family members are professional editors with a strong grasp of the English language, I advise against this.

When I asked my own good friends for help with this, I got so many conflicting point of views that it paralyzed me. You can always request feedbacks and comments from your friends, however it's better to have a professional editor for a professional outcome.

Working with an editor does not need to be expensive. My editors only demand me $5 for every 250 words (I was able to bargain such a reduced price due to the fact that I've hired them on for a multiple projects). For a 14,000- word composition that's a total amount of only $56.

You don't need to employ two editors like I do, yet you do need to hire at least one!

You're already spending a lot energy and time right into your book. Why not invest $50-$100 to obtain professional editing so that it reads well as well as obtains excellent assessments? Your investment will certainly pay off in raised sales.

Creating Your Editing Team

Since you know exactly how essential it is to have a editing group, you could be questioning how you can hire a professional to help you. If you have not currently built a team of Kindle editors and also designers, you'll have to begin to hunt for an editor. The best two resources for hiring editors are Elance (https://www.elance.com/) and oDesk (https://www.odesk.com/). Both are good sources and offer competitive rates.

To hire an editor on Elance, you'll log into your Elance account and create a new job. Here's the job template I use:

Edit My 15,000 Word EBook

I'm searching for someone to edit my upcoming eBook. The editor should have a solid grasp of the English language and a tested performance history. You must have the ability to deal with grammar, spelling mistake and change the sentences to make them flow a lot better.

The eBook is short - less than 15,000 words.

I'm seeking top quality editing at a low, affordable price. Reply with the words "Blue Sky" in your reply so I recognize you've read this task description.

What's your ideal price?

I consistently bring in the expression "reply with words 'Blue Sky' in your reply so that I recognize you've checked out the work description." I do this to narrow down freelancers to those that have actually read through the description.

Some freelancers will certainly bid for your work without truly reviewing the description. You don't want that sort of editor for your book.

As soon as you make your task live, you'll begin obtaining proposals. You could quickly weed out anybody who does not utilize your secret language in his or her reply. You want a person with focus on information for your editing job.

You will certainly be left with many freelancers. You should go through each profile and check out reviews. While it may appear unjust to brand-new freelancers, I simply work those that have a tried and tested track record.

I search for freelancers which have at the very least 10 tasks under their belt with at least a 95 % favorable evaluation rating (some bad testimonials are expected, specifically when a freelancer has a bunch of jobs under his or her belt). These are my criteria and also you're free to choose your very own - however this is a great system if you're new to outsourcing.

Since you've narrowed it down much more, you would like to test their work with a little task. I select exactly what I assume are the leading 3 bids as well as send them a message stating I 'd like to examine their services before I provide a full job.

For this, I bargain a rate of $1 for 250 words and send out a 1,000-word document to edit. This winds up being $4 per freelancer. Certainly, not everyone approves this price, so you have to negotiate. When I acquire samples back, I take a look at the high quality as well as select the freelancer that I feel did the very best task.

I likewise prefer to work with a 2nd editor to look at the book after the very first editor, merely to confirm that there aren't any sorts of mistakes.

Avoid Hiring Editors From Fiverr

Fiverr is an outstanding source for some solutions such as graphic design. However it doesn't appear to provide the exact same top quality when it involves editors. I have actually tried numerous editors from Fiverr but have actually been dissatisfied by their quality.

It seems like a great site to employ an individual and save cash, but with editing you obtain just what you spend for. Do not hesitate to experiment. Nevertheless, make sure to constantly test editors with a shorter piece of text.

Editing Results

After you send your book off to an editor, it could take 2-3 days to get it returned. I have a good working relationship with my editors and also obtain priority treatment. Yet, this could require time to establish.

When you get your book back, check it. If you really feel that it requires even more work, do not hesitate to send it back and request more specifics regarding just what you still need.

Editing Tasks

The main tasks you require for this part of your book development consist of:

1. Employing an editor team if you don't already have one in position.

2. Sending your book off to be edited.

3. Assessing edits and also sending it back once more if required.

You'll have a few days between sending the book and also getting it back.

Chapter 9
FORMATTING YOUR KINDLE EBOOK

Many self published authors have lost a lot of hair with the process of Kindle formatting – that's for sure. But you won't, because you've got me and I will certainly make this process a piece of cake for you. Now you won't need to spend extra bucks for formatting your book. This is if you have a good knowledge of using basic features in MS Word like paragraph styles, page breaks, automatic TOC, etc. If not, I would recommend you not to do this on your own or better you could learn these features once and for all and format your own books easily.

I have created a standard template design in MS Word just for you. All you have to do is replace the dummy content in the Template with your own content and you are done with formatting. Yes it's that easy.

Formatting your book for kindle is all about following some simple rules using which I have created a template for you. Just remember the following rules and you should do just fine:

- Use the default heading styles available in MS Word instead of manually editing the font of your content each time.

- Don't use the Enter Key to adjust spacing between two chapters to adjust them on a new page. If you want anything to start on the next page, use Page Break instead.

- Use an Auto Generated Table of Contents instead of writing it yourself. Another amazing feature available in Microsoft Word. After you are done replacing the template with your own content, just right click on the table of contents and select Update field and it should replace the table of contents with your own.

- For this to work properly, the heading of all your chapters must be in Heading 1 Style, Sub chapters in Heading 2 Style and if you have further sub sections, you can continue to put them in Heading 3 and 4. The main content or the body of your chapters must be in Normal Style.

- If want to add images to your book, use the 'Insert Image' option. Do not copy-paste the images directly into word file.

- Finally, remember to make sure that after you paste your content in the template, it is pasted with the destination formatting, that is, the formatting styles in the template and not with the formatting style of the original content source.

Check out this link to get your free template: https://www.dropbox.com/s/6c9wd6f0joifg3q/kindle-template.docx?dl=0

.